ANGRY

by Rochelle Nielsen Barsuhn
illustrated by
Kathryn Hutton

Distributed by
Standard Publishing,
Cincinnati, Ohio 45231.

ELGIN, ILLINOIS 60120

Note to parents and teachers:

Feelings are genuine responses to life situations. Sometimes our feelings are appropriate to those situations. Sometimes they are not. Regardless, we need to accept our feelings and direct expressions of feeling positively if we hope to be effective Christian witnesses.

The feelings of children are intense. There is beauty in that. And there is promise. But in the expression of feeling, problems sometimes arise. Uncontrolled or misdirected expression of negative feeling can be harmful.

This book presents a number of situations that can cause anger. Use these situations to promote discussion. Help children identify positive outlets for their anger in actions that will help, rather than harm, themselves and others.

Most situations in which we find ourselves contain humor. Sometimes children see that best.

Distributed by Standard Publishing, 8121 Hamilton Avenue, Cincinnati, Ohio 45231.

Library of Congress Cataloging in Publication Data

Barsuhn, Rochelle Nielsen, 1958-
   Angry.

  (What does it mean?)
  Summary: Presents several situations that can cause anger, and suggests positive outlets for anger in helpful, rather than harmful, actions.
   1. Anger—Juvenile literature. [1. Anger]
I. Hutton, Kathryn. II. Title. III. Series.
BF575.A5B37 1982   152.4   82-4570
ISBN 0-89565-234-X   AACR2

© 1982 The Child's World, Inc.
All rights reserved. Printed in U.S.A.

1 2 3 4 5 6 7 8 9 10 11 12 R 89 88 87 86 85 84 83 82

ANGRY

"If you are angry, don't sin by nursing your grudge. Don't let the sun go down with you still angry—get over it quickly."

—Ephesians 4:26 [TLB]

When you were a child, Lord,
you played with your friends.

Sometimes my friends and I disagree.
Sometimes we fight.
If I make people laugh instead of cry
then you will be happy. And so will I.

—Madeleine L'Engle

Copyright Madeleine L'Engle,
published by Morehouse-Barlow Co., Inc.
Used by permission.

When someone is mean to me, I GET ANGRY

Bullies are mean.
They knock me down.
They push me on the ground
and run.

I cry.
I yell, "You dumb-dumb!"
and chase them.
When I catch one,
I'll push him in the snow
and run.

But then
I'll be a dumb-dumb too.

Lydia promised
to play with me.

But when recess came,
she went to climb the jungle gym
with Ellen.
"You promised!" I said.

But Lydia and Ellen
are hanging by their knees
from the jungle gym.
And I'm angry,
swinging by myself.

Sarah broke
the golden crayon I used
to color rings, kings, and rainbows.

She's not sorry.
She thinks it's funny.

I don't.
I want to break
something of hers.

Instead,
I breathe deeply.

"Sarah," I say, "I'm angry."

Sometimes when things
don't go my way,
I GET ANGRY

"Pick up
 those paints
  before you play."

I knew Grandpa meant what he said.

"But Andrea's here.
 You said I could play."

Grandpa looked at me, shaking his head.

I went to the bedroom
to pick up the paints.

I was mad,
but I did what he said.

As I set up the game
to play again,
Mom said, "It's time for bed now."

I was
      a little
           tired, but . . .
I wanted to play, not sleep!

I felt like crying.
Instead, I hollered
    from the top of the stairs,
"I don't like bed,
    and I don't like you."
Then Mom was angry too.

She came upstairs
and talked with me.
"Sorry I was mean," I said.

It's raining
big splashing drops
even though the whole grade
packed chips and sandwiches
for our spring picnic.

It's no one's fault,
but I want to yell and shout.
Rain spoils picnics.

Lunch is at noon
but I'm hungry now.
That soggy breakfast cereal I ate
won't get me through jump rope
    and cardboard forts.
It makes me angry
that I have to wait.
"I can't!" I say to Mom.
My voice growls like my stomach . . .

    LUNCH!

    Funny how
    after the first bite
    of peanut butter
    the world seems better,
    and I don't growl.

Mom and Dad left
Randall in charge.
Randall's my brother.
He's older.

Randall wanted to watch TV—
a very, very,
    long, long,
        old, old
            movie.
He wouldn't even listen
to what I wanted to do.

"I'm going to tell,"
I said and shut the door
on Randall
and the TV.

When I don't do what I should, OTHERS GET ANGRY

Today I watched cartoons
and didn't clean my room.

Dad is angry
because there's dust
and one half-eaten Twinkie under my bed.
I'd rather watch Bugs Bunny
than clean, but
I pick up my toys
and make the bed
and throw that Twinkie in the garbage.
"Dad," I say, "I'm sorry."

Now cartoons will be more fun
and so will Dad.

I made fun of Marvin.
Marvin has mumps.
"You look like a chipmunk," I laughed.
(I saw one once.
Its cheeks were stuffed with nuts.)

But Marvin didn't laugh.
"I do not!" he said.
He frowned at me from his bed,
piled high with toys
and our grey cat.

I didn't mean to make him mad,
so
I brought him ice cream.

When I'm not happy with myself,
I GET ANGRY

My sister's hair is curly.
Mine's straight.
She's good at everything,
even art.

Everyone likes her pictures.
So I get angry
when I can't draw
mud-brown horses like she can.

When I tell Dad,
he smiles.
"You're better in math.
Besides,
your hair is thick
and a beautiful black!"

Today wasn't easy, Lord.
I'm mad at everybody—
Mom,
Dad,
Gramps,
and
Betsy (who's my very best friend).
I feel mean.

Telling You helps.
I don't feel so bad now.
And I'm not even mad
anymore.

                      Amen.

About the Author:

Rochelle Nielsen Barsuhn studied English literature at Bethel College (St. Paul, Minnesota). Her written work has appeared in several magazines for children. Ms. Barsuhn describes herself as "a reader of books—children's, the classics, and anything in print." Currently, she works with her husband in their Minneapolis-based design and advertising agency.

About the Artist:

Kathryn Hutton graduated from Berea College in Kentucky and attended the Cincinnati (Ohio) Art Academy. She has been a commercial artist for 40 years. Mrs. Hutton particularly likes to draw children and through the years she has used her four children and four grandchildren for inspiration. She resides in "non-retirement" in Fairfield, Ohio.